CHRISTOPHER D. RODKEY,
JESSE & NATALIE TURRI

COLORING ADVENT

An Adult Coloring Book for the
Journey to Bethlehem

CBP

ST. LOUIS, MISSOURI

COLORING ADVENT

TABLE OF CONTENTS

CRIB NOTES FROM BETHLEHEM:
A THEOLOGICAL INTRODUCTION[1]

> *But when the fullness of time had come, God sent his Son, born of a woman, born under the law,*
> *in order to redeem those who were under the law, so that we might receive adoption as children.*
> *And because you are children, God has sent the Spirit of his Son into our hearts, crying, "Abba!*
> *Father!" So you are no longer a slave but a child, and if a child then also an heir, through God.*
>
> *Galatians 4:4-7 (NRSV)*

These words of Paul are probably everything we need to theologically know about Christmas in just a few sentences, that God submits to the logic of sacrifice to undo the logic of sacrifice, to be sacrificed on the cross by entering human form, and submitting to the law or logic of humanity. As a result, we are all children of the same divine parent: no longer slaves to the ways of the world but heirs to inherit the Kingdom of God by building the Kingdom of God for ourselves and for future generations.

Has this ever been realized? Have we ever realized the brotherhood and sisterhood of humanity in our time? Have we ever found a way to subvert the system of violence and crucifixion that this world has known? Many of our nations and much of humanity may believe that we have achieved this first step of bringing peace on earth and goodwill to humankind, but we know we have really cheated the full sense of what it means to acknowledge that God is born in a manger.

There is something special about the Christmas carol "Away in a Manger."

When we sing that as a lullaby to children, we sometimes miss that when we sing the song, we are, in essence, ordaining them to lead us, as children, to become bearers of the Christ-child.

What would this world be like if we recognized the Christhood and the Godhood present in the new flesh of babies and children, and honored the sacredness of this humanity God has come to save? With the number of children living in poverty and hunger in our country and everywhere in the world, we have not only turned our backs upon the world; we have turned our backs upon God-made-flesh. Stated more accurately, the behavior of this world has in fact stolen the divinity and sacredness of cribs of unsuspecting children throughout the world.

A first step for us to move forward is to recognize that we too have had our Christhood stolen from the crib. We too are victims of this world even as we participate in the victimization of the world. The God-who-is-made-known-to-us-in-newborn-flesh is God-with-us and God-in-us, God living and breathing and perishing with us.

If the Christ-child has been abducted from our lives, the time has arrived to return it to our hearts, and to our spirits. If we have cheated in responding to the Good News of Christmas, it is now time to rectify our commitment to the Kingdom of God, whose birth pangs are ringing loudly around us in Christmas bells, festive lights, and carols, and in anticipation of the Christhood delivered to us as a child being born on this dark and cold night.

Christopher D. Rodkey

Notes

1. I have cribbed this title from Laurel Schneider's excellent essay of the same title, "Crib Notes from Bethlehem," in *Polydoxy: Theology of Multiplicity and Relation*, ed. Catherine Keller and Laurel Schneider (New York: Routledge, 2011): 19-35. This essay is adapted from Christopher Rodkey, *The World is Crucifixion: Radical Christian Preaching, Year C* (Aurora, CO: Noesis, 2016), 41-42.

God Enters The World

AUTUMNAL EPIGRAPH

When the fullness of time arrives, God enters the world as a cloud descending upon the flesh of a woman, so that we might all receive the same Holy Spirit and the entire world will call upon God as our universal Parent.

Galatians 4

Celestial Innocence

OPENING PRAYER

May You set Your openness toward my inwardness, so I might know who I am by knowing You. And in this knowing, may what had been closed in Adam become newly opened in me.

As You entered Your servant, the Celestial Virgin, the angels were stunned in surprise. This is the greatest miracle of all time, and could only have been accomplished by divine love.

May such celestial innocence be granted to me and to Your church in this journey of awaiting Your return into the world. May the laughter of angels echo in the the highest heavens and into the pit once again as we take up the cross of the Virgin and become bearers of the Christ, now and into the world yet to be birthed.

Amen.

After Jacob Böhme†

The Secret

ADVENT DAY 1

The mysteries of long ago, the mysteries of the present, and the mysteries of the future converge in our story of God's entrance into the world. The secret is about to be known as we begin this journey of Advent.

Romans 16

Pouring Out Into History

ADVENT DAY 2

God speaks though our history and our
ancestors through clouds, fire, and prophets.
If we study this history closely enough, God is
found continually pouring out new entrances
into the world everywhere we look.

Hebrews 1

The Logos

ADVENT DAY 3

The universe is created with a prioritization of justice,
through the Word spoken by the Cloud.

Psalm 145, John 1†

Nathan Speaks

ADVENT DAY 4

God speaks through the prophet Nathan, instructing him to tell King David that God will always be with them, and that the Cloud will cascade among God's people.

2 Samuel 7

Ethan Sings

ADVENT DAY 5

God again speaks to King David through his court musician, Ethan. Ethan sings to the King a reassurance that the Cloud continues to arrive to God's people and that a young one will be raised from the people to demonstrate the love God has for this people.

Psalm 89

David Prays

ADVENT DAY 6

King David prays to God, thanking God for loving everyone, and for always keeping promises.

Psalm 25

Earth Fills With the Cloud

ADVENT DAY 7

King David's son, King Solomon, sings a prayer to God, proclaiming that the earth will be filled with the Cloud of God.

Psalm 72

Baruch Writes

ADVENT DAY 8

Later, when God's people are taken into captivity away from their home, the scribe of the prophet Jeremiah, Baruch ben Neriah, writes to the people to wait for God to enter the world, bringing joy, glory, mercy, and righteousness.

Baruch 5†

Justice

ADVENT DAY 9

The vision of the prophet Isaiah: The justice of God
will be established and there will be peace on earth.

Isaiah 2

Hope

ADVENT DAY 10

Isaiah and Jeremiah share a
vision that a new hope will
arise out of the tree of Jesse.

Isaiah 11, Jeremiah 33

Saint Nicholas

INTERRUPTION:
ST. NICHOLAS
KONTAKION

St. Nicholas, you priestly worker in Myra:

you zealously lived the Gospel of Christ;

you dedicated your life to God's people;

you saved the innocent from death.

In these ways you are clothed in holiness

as a great mystic of God's grace.

As it is written:

"By his words he performed swift miracles;

the Lord glorified him in the

presence of kings…

He allowed him to hear his voice,

And led him into the dark cloud."

(Sirach 45:3, 5 NRSV)

Amen.†

Stars Will Fall

ADVENT DAY 11

Isaiah calls upon God to descend from the heavens like a star falling to the earth.

A red dragon, from a distance, watches. And waits.

Isaiah 64 , Revelation 12

Malachi Prophesies

ADVENT DAY 12

The prophet Malachi also predicts that a messenger will arrive who will prepare the highway for the Cloud to enter the world.

Malachi 3

A Prayer For Uninhibited Spirit

ADVENT DAY 13

Lead us to not bow to the gods of fear, but rather lead us to embody the wildness of the Holy Spirit, boldly and intolerably deviating from the profanity of this world. May we speak with tongues of fire that echo the words of prophets and ancestors until we see in our midst Your peace. *Amen.*

1 Thessalonians 5

The Fullness of Time

ADVENT DAY 14

Let us keep watch for God to saturate this world, but not with our own expectations. For no one knows when or how, but the Cloud will come in the fullness of time, unexpectedly, and surprisingly—like a thief who interrupts the night. *Amen.*

Matthew 24, Mark 13, Luke 21, 2 Peter 3

New Life Is Teeming

ADVENT DAY 15

Like a farmer who is patient with early and late rains upon her crops, may we be patient in like manner, for the day of new life is about to commence. *Amen.*

James 5, Luke 21

Kenosis

ADVENT DAY 16

In the day of the coming of the Lord, the heavens will dissolve
and all of creation will melt into something entirely new, and the
love of the Cloud will pour out into the world.

2 Peter 3

Be Prepared

ADVENT DAY 17

The night is now behind us; only the day lies before us. Now is the moment to awake from our sleep, for God is about to enter the world.

Romans 13†

Joseph Is Awakened

ADVENT DAY 18

An Angel of the Cloud visits Joseph and tells
him that Mary, whom he loves, will have a baby.

Matthew 1

The Annunciation

ADVENT DAY 19

The angel Gabriel visits Mary and tells Mary not to be afraid, and that she will have a baby.

Luke 1

The Canticle of Mary

ADVENT DAY 20

Mary offers consent and sings a song of
love: God loves everyone, and loves
everyone so much that the Cloud of
love will enter the world through
her own womb.

Luke 1†

Gaudete!

INTERLUDE
(EMBER DAY 1)

Gaudete! Gaudete!

The time of grace we have desired is now;

Let us sing songs of joy and offer devotion.

God is made flesh, and nature stands in amazement;

The world is renewed, as in this womb is a king.

The locked door of Ezekiel is shattered!

Let our assembly sing the Psalms to purify us;

Let our church praise the Cloud

Now hidden in Mary's Womb!

Gaudete!

Traditional Latin Carol†

The Visitation

ADVENT DAY 21

Mary visits her cousin Elizabeth, who is pregnant with a baby named John, and the babies jump for joy inside of their bodies.

Luke 1

Es Ist Ein Ros Entsprungen

INTERRUPTION
(EMBER DAY 2)

Lo, how a rose e'er blooming
from Jesse's graceful root.

As the ancient prophets sang, it came
in the cold winter,
in the middle of the night.

This Rose of which Isaiah
sang was beheld by Mary,

Who has born a child
who makes us blessed,
in the night.

This rose, so tender,
whose fragrance is sweet,

With its light the darkness recedes,
and saves us from death.

Traditional German Carol†

The Baptist

ADVENT DAY 22

Later, as an adult, Elizabeth's son, John, would stand near the Jordan River, proclaiming that God's work of creation and ongoing New Creation is far from completion.

Matthew 3†

Praecursor Altus Luminis

INTERRUPTION
(EMBER DAY 3)

The great forerunner of the morn,
The herald of the Word is born:
And faithful hearts shall never fail
With thanks and praise his light to hail.

John, still unborn, yet gave aright
His witness to the coming Light;
And Christ, the sun of all the earth,
Fulfilled that witness at His birth.

But why should mortal accents raise
The hymn of John the Baptist's praise?
Of whom, or e'er his course was run,
Thus spake the Cloud through the sun?

"Behold, My herald, who shall go
Before Thy face Thy way to show,
And shine, as with the day-star's gleam,
Before Thine own eternal Beam."

After St. Bede
as translated by John M. Neale†

The Census

ADVENT DAY 23

Caesar Augustus wants to know how many people live in area, so he makes everyone return to their hometowns. Mary and Joseph must travel to return home.

Luke 2

Emergency Stop

ADVENT DAY 24

Mary and Joseph travel, and when the Cloud is in position, they stop in Bethlehem. Finding no room at an inn, they are offered shelter with the animals. When their son is born, they lay him in a manger.

Luke 2

Shepherds' Watch

ADVENT DAY 25

An angel visits the shepherds, who are with their flocks outside of the town. The angel tells them to not be afraid: *the Cloud is about to descend.*

Luke 2

The Star Descends

ADVENT DAY 26

Wise men from far away have been watching for Isaiah's star to come down. The star descends, and they travel to Jerusalem looking for God's entrance in the world. Not finding God there, they follow the star out of the city.

Matthew 2

Self-Negation

ADVENT DAY 27

God is now about to pour Godself into the world in the most impossible and improbable of ways! Not from the station of the rich, but through a poor child. Not from a line of sitting royalty, but from a family of sinners. Not from a station of political or religious power, but in the weakness of a baby. Not from heaven, but from the flesh of earth.

Isaiah 61, Matthew 1, Luke 3, Philippians 2

Prefiguring Pietá

CHRISTMAS EVE

Jesus is born, Cloud enfleshed, in a manger. Mary
loved her baby, and knew that God loved her.

Luke 2

Birth of God

CHRISTMAS DAY

God is born newly in our world, and will establish a world of justice and peace!

Let the heavens rejoice! Let the earth be glad! All creation rejoices!

Through the Christ-child, God is poured out upon us, and born through us.

Isaiah 9, Psalms 96-98, Titus 3

The Shepherd's Arrival

CHRISTMASTIDE DAY 2 (DECEMBER 26)

The shepherds visit the baby Jesus, and they tell everyone that God has entered the world.

Luke 2

The Holy Name

CHRISTMASTIDE DAY 3 (DECEMBER 27)

Joseph adopts Mary's child, and names him Jesus.

Matthew 1, Luke 2†

The Circumcision

CHRISTMASTIDE DAY 4 (DECEMBER 28)

After being named, Jesus is circumcised—an act that, only a few generations ago, would have led to the execution of any involved in the ritual if discovered by the authorities.

While being marked in accordance with tradition,
the first blood of Jesus is shed for the world.

1 Maccabees 1, Luke 1, Luke 2†

The Presentation

CHRISTMASTIDE DAY 5 (DECEMBER 29)

Again following the custom of their time, Mary and Joseph bring the baby Jesus to the Temple to be presented with a sacrificial offering of two turtledoves. To the amazement of the young parents, two prophets, Simeon and Anna, know as soon as they see baby Jesus that He is the Messiah.

Luke 2†

Herod's Conspiracy

CHRISTMASTIDE DAY 6 (DECEMBER 30)

King Herod, having heard that the Messiah had arrived, feels threatened and summons the star-following wise men. Herod asks them to return to him with the location of the baby.

Matthew 2

The Magi's Gifts

CHRISTMASTIDE DAY 7 (DECEMBER 31)

Leaving Herod, the wise men follow the star, leading them to the baby Jesus.

Arriving to see the young family and knowing who Jesus is, the wise men offer him gifts: gold, symbolizing the royalty of Jesus; frankincense, acknowledging his priestly role; and myrrh, an embalming agent representing the importance of Jesus' eventual death.

Matthew 2

They Are Wise Men

CHRISTMASTIDE DAY 8 (JANUARY 1)

In a dream, the wise men receive a warning not to trust Herod, and they depart from Bethlehem, returning home by a different path.

Matthew 2

The Holy Family

CHRISTMASTIDE DAY 9 (JANUARY 2)

Angels speak to Joseph in a dream, warning him of King Herod's hatred for his son. In the middle of the night, he awakens Mary, and they flee to Egypt. The Holy Family remain there until an angel advises Joseph to return to their hometown of Nazareth.

Matthew 2†

Infanticide

CHRISTMASTIDE DAY 10 (JANUARY 3)

Outraged that the wise men have tricked him, King Herod orders all children in Bethlehem aged two and under to be executed.. The cries of horror and lamentation fill the streets and pierce the heavens.

Matthew 2†

The Doctors In The Temple

CHRISTMASTIDE DAY 11 (JANUARY 4)

After Herod dies, the Holy Family returns to Nazareth and there lead fairly uneventful lives until Jesus is twelve. While traveling home from Jerusalem after the Passover, his parents notice that he is missing, and they return to the city to look for him.

After three days of searching, they find Jesus in the Temple, sitting with the other teachers and learning, discussing, and interpreting the Torah. The others are astonished at his knowledge and insight.

Jesus says to his parents, "Why did you not know to find me here, in my Father's house?"
The Holy Family again returns together to Nazareth.

Luke 2

The Crucifixion of Mary

CHRISTMASTIDE
DAY 12
(JANUARY 5)

Jesus grows big and strong, and the Cloud surrounds him.

But looking back upon the events of Jesus' birth and childhood, Mary enshrines the words of recognition by others in her heart; pondering, questioning, rehearsing, and worrying.

For Mary knows the fate of the cross her child must suffer. And this is her ongoing crucifixion.

Luke 2

Prayer of Implosion

THE EPIPHANY
(JANUARY 6)

God has shattered transcendence
through an entrance into flesh.

And how will I respond?

Even while darkness has covered the
earth, light recedes from the darkness.

Injustice and violence may finally
become untangled from humanity.

How will I respond?

Will I celebrate feast days and fast
days? Will I invent new sacred games?

Or will I bring gifts to the Christ
child?

Will I honor the sanctity of human
life?

Will I bring gifts of gold, frankincense,
and myrrh to God's children?

Arise, for the Light shines. It is time
to make my decision.

Amen.

Psalm 72, Isaiah 60, Matthew 2

Sol Invictus

POSTSCRIPT: THE SOLEMNITY OF MARY

The Cloud investitures Mary with the sun, and coronates her with stars, as she stands upon the three stages of the moon.

The red dragon, after pulling down a third of all the stars in search, finally discovers Mary, wanting to find the Star who had escaped him, whom she held nursing in her arms.

But the Star Child was spirited away to be hidden in the darkness of Cloud, and Mary escapes into the wilderness.

Revelation 12†

Home By A Different Road

THE BENEDICTION

Shout and rejoice with joy! For God has entered flesh!

The Cloud has descended and has come to smash the injustice of this world!

The shame of the leper and the marginalized will be reversed;

May the Christ lead you home by a different road! *Amen.*

Isaiah 12, Zephaniah 3

Opening Prayer: Celestial Innocence

Jacob Böhme, *Three Principles* (§xviii, 42), as quoted in Franz Hartmann, *The Life and Doctrine of Jacob Boehme* (London: Paul and Trench, 1891), 242.

Jacob Böhme (1575-1624) was a noted Christian esotericist and mystic.

Advent Day 3: The Logos

"The arc of the universe is long but it bends toward justice" is a famous quote by Unitarian minister Theodore Parker (1810-1860), in his *Ten Sermons on Religion* in 1853, although it is often attributed to Albert Pike (1809-1891); Martin Luther King, Jr. (1929-1968); and Barack Obama (1961-).

Advent Day 8: Baruch Writes

The Book of Baruch is part of the Old Testament canon of Catholicism and is considered a deuterocanonical text by most Protestants. The lection employed on this page, Baruch 5:1-9, appears in the Catholic lectionary on Year C, Advent 2.

Interruption: St. Nicholas *Kontakion*

A "kontakion" is a kind of liturgical hymn used in the Eastern Orthodox and Byzantine Catholic Churches. This particular kontakion is adapted from a Byzantine Rite hymn.

The Feast of St. Nicholas is observed on Dec. 6 by Western Churches and Dec. 19 by Eastern Churches, celebrating the life of the historical St. Nicholas of Myra (270-343 CE). The deuterocanonical Sirach 45:3 is a common liturgical reading for St. Nicholas Day.

Advent Day 17: Be Prepared

Here I make reference to Friedrich Nietzsche's apprehension before his madman's declaration of the death of God; see Nietzsche, *The Gay Science*, trans. W. Kaufmann (New York: Vintage, 1974), §124.

Advent Day 20: The Canticle of Mary

While I deeply appreciate Mary Daly's radical feminist critique of the Virgin Mary in her phenomenal book, *Pure Lust* (Boston: Beacon, 1984) as an archetype of sexual assault; I take Mary's answer as offering consent. The Greek Luke 1:38b, "γένοιτό μοι κατὰ τὸ ῥῆμά σου," contains the unusual form of γένοιτό—aorist optative middle, third-person singular—that is, "let it be" as contractual language. My interpretation is that Luke intentionally offered this subtle hint to his first-century readers to differentiate his story from discourses of abuse found in comparative Greek mythology.

Interlude: *Gaudete!* (Ember Day 1)

According to the traditional liturgical cycle, "Ember Days" four times per year in sets of three days in the course of one week—celebrated Wednesday, Friday, and Saturday. They are presented here as an interlude in conjunction with the narrative themes of this work. The "Embertide" or sequence of Ember Days in the season of Advent would traditionally be observed in the "Ember Week" between the third and fourth Sundays of the season (for Anglicans, the Ember Week is held between the second and third Sundays of Advent).

Ember Days are special days of abstinence, fasting, and penance, and are the time for the sacrament of the ordination of priests.

The first Ember Day in Advent is traditionally associated with the Annunciation, and its lection is Luke 1:26-38.

"Gaudete" is a traditional Latin carol whose origins are unknown; "Gaudete" means "rejoice." Its first publication was in 1582 in *Piae Cantiones*, a hymn collection of 74 Latin songs well-known in Finland. Presented here is my minimalistic, thematic, and loose translation.

Interlude: *Es ist ein Ros entsprungen* (Ember Day 2)

The Second "Ember Day" observed in Advent focuses upon the Visitation of Mary and Elizabeth (Luke 1:37-47).

"Es ist ein Ros entsprungen" is best known in English as "Lo, How a Rose E'er Blooming," a hymn based on Isaiah 11:1. The original author is unknown, with additional lyrics added by Friedrich Layriz (1808-1859). Translations into English found today are by Catharine Winkworth (1827-1878) and Theodore Baker (1851-1934). My presentation is a loose presentation of the German and the better-known English translations.

Advent Day 22: The Baptist

This story sits well outside of the timeline of events but it is presented here to emphasize that the lectionary cycle places this story in the season of Advent. Since Advent is not only waiting for Jesus to arrive, it is a "waiting" for the arrival of Christ at all times in history—whether we speak of days of the annunciation, the Baptist, Holy Saturday, or this day.

Interlude: *Praecursor altus luminis* (Ember Day 3)

The Third "Ember Day" celebrated in Advent is typically focused upon John the Baptist and the reading for the day is Luke 3:1-6.

"Praecursor altus luminis" is an ancient hymn by "The Venerable" St. Bede (673?-735 CE) and was translated into English as "The Great Forerunner of the Morn" by noted hymnist John M. Neale (1818-1866), published in his *Hymnal Noted, Parts I & II* (London: Novello, 1851), no. 97 (p. 189-190). I have slightly modified the text and have included the first, third, fourth, and fifth of the six verses of the hymn. The lection Isaiah 49:1 is noted with the hymn.

Christmastide Day 3 (December 27): The Holy Name

The Feast of the Holy Name of Jesus is celebrated on different dates by churches, but is most prominently observed on January 1. An important historical spiritual practice is the devotion and dedication of the name, Jesus, which is emphasized on this day.

Christmastide Day 4 (December 28): The Circumcision

During the rule of the Syrian King Antiochus IV over Judea—according to the apocryphal 1 Maccabees 1:60-61— if discovered, a circumcised child and those involved in his circumcision would be put to death and the dead child would be hung around the neck of the mother.

The Feast of the Circumcision of Christ is held on the eighth day of Christmastide, January 1, though it appears earlier in our narrative story. One Eastern tradition is that the foreskin of Christ was kept in an alabaster jar of spikenard, and was the same jar that would appear later in Matthew 26:7 and Luke 7:37. This story is mixed with the coloring page in *Coloring Lent*, Day 22.

Christmastide Day 5 (December 29): The Presentation

The Presentation of Jesus in the Temple is a Great Feast of Eastern Orthodoxy, usually remembered on February 2. Although associated with the season of Epiphany, the historical sequence places it here in our narrative.

Christmastide Day 9 (January 2): The Holy Family

The Feast of the Holy Family is observed on the first Sunday of Christmastide if it falls between Christmas Day and New Year's Day. Otherwise it is designated for December 30. It is a day of presenting the Holy Family as a model of the Christian family. In this tradition, I depict the family as displaced refugees.

Christmastide Day 10 (January 3): Infanticide

The Holy Innocents' Day or "Childermas" is celebrated by the Western churches on December 28. In the Caribbean some countries use this day to bless the toys of children. For me, it is an important remembrance of those who are victims and survivors of miscarriage and pregnancy loss.

Postscript: The Solemnity of Mary, *Sol Invictus*

"Sol invictus" is a term with a long history of being related to sun gods; in Latin it means "unconquered sun." Following tradition, I interpret the woman of Revelation 12 to be Mary and the red dragon to represent empire, from which Jesus and Mary escape for now. In working through this image I am particularly fond of Jan L. Richardson's depiction of Mary in "Her Glorious Robe," in *Night Visions* (Cleveland: Pilgrim, 1998), 76-77.

SCRIPTURE REFERENCES

LECTIONARY INDEX

Year C

Advent

First Sunday...................................... Advent Days 6, 10, 14, 15
Second Sunday................................. Advent Days 8, 12
Third Sunday.................................... Benediction
Fourth Sunday................................. Advent Days 20, 21;
          Ember Day 2

Christmastide

Nativity, prop. 1................................ Advent Days 23, 24, 25;
          Christmas Eve;
          Christmas Day;
          Christmastide Day 12
Nativity, prop. 2................................ Advent Days 23, 24, 25;
          Christmas Eve;
          Christmas Day;
          Christmastide Days 2, 12
Nativity, prop. 3................................ Advent Days 2, 3;
          Christmas Day

Epiphany

Epiphany... Advent Days 7, 26;
          Christmastide Days 6, 7, 8, 9;
          Epiphany
Ninth Sunday .... Christmas Day

Lent

Liturgy of the Passion .... Advent Day 27
Holy Tuesday.................................... Ember Day 3

Easter

Easter Vigil .... Benediction

Season after Pentecost

Proper 10 .... Advent Day 6
Proper 27 .... Christmas Day
Proper 28 .... Christmas Day; Benediction
Thanksgiving (USA & Canada)...... Benediction

Special Observances Excluded Above

- Feast of St. Nicholas (Dec. 6): St. Nicholas *Kontakion*
- Advent Ember Week: Ember Days 1, 2, 3
- Feast of the Holy Innocents (Dec. 28): Christmastide Day 10
- Feast of the Holy Family: Christmastide Day 9
- Solemnity of the Blessed Virgin Mary (Jan. 1): Christmastide Day 12; Postscript
- Memorial of the Holy Name of Jesus (Jan. 4): Epigraph; Advent Day 27; Christmastide Days 2, 3, 4, 12
- Feast of the Three Kings (Jan. 6): Advent Day 26; Christmastide Days 7, 8
- Feast of the Baptism of the Lord: Advent Day 22
- Feast of the Presentation of the Lord (Feb. 2): Christmastide Days 9, 12
- Solemnity of St. Joseph (March 19): Advent Day 18
- The Annunciation of the Lord (March 25): Advent Days 19, 20; Ember Day 1, 2
- Feast of the Visitation of Mary (May 31): Advent Day 21, Ember Day 2
- Nativity of St. John the Baptist (June 24): Advent Day 21, Ember Day 3
- Feast of St. Mary (Sept. 8): Advent Day 20; Ember Day 2; Advent Days 23, 24; Christmas Eve; Christmas Day; Christmastide Day 12; Postscript
- Feast of the Archangels (Sept. 29): Advent Days 18, 19, 25
- Thanksgiving (all years): Epigraph

THE *VIA MATRIS*: THE SEVEN SORROWS OF MARY

The Seven Sorrows is a way of reflection, typically with a rosary or chaplet, upon the life of Christ from the perspective of Mary. The goal of this ancient practice is to journey the via matris, or "the way of the mother," who "treasured" the signs and wonders of Jesus' childhood "and pondered them in her heart" (Luke 2:19 NRSV).